THE JARED LINE

By Nan Jared Powell

Sons of James Allison Jared:
Marvin Wilcox(L), Porter Alexander(R), and Daniel Wade(M)

The Jared Line

By Nan Jared Powell

Copyright © 2019 Nan Powell

ISBN 978-1-939696-51-9

REF013000 REFERENCE / Genealogy & Heraldry

Cover by: Resa Reid

Pictured on the front cover from left to right:

David James Jared

Edmond F. Jared, Sr.

Nan Jared Powell

Edmond F. Jared, Jr.

Jerry Harrell Jared

Dedication

Dedicated with love to my father and mother, Edmond Feris and Charlotte Celeste Harrell Jared.

Papa and Nonnie

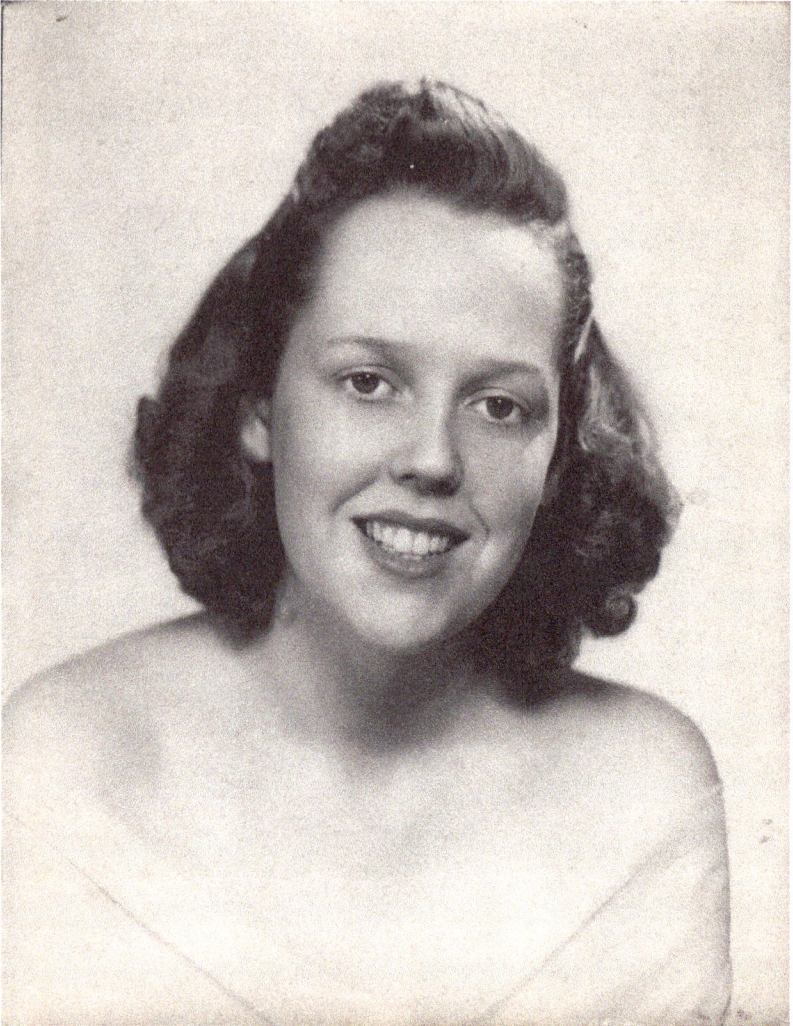

Charlotte Celeste Harrell Jared

A native of Adel, Georgia, Celeste had lived in Gainsville since 1946. She was the daughter of Steven and Dassie Jones Harrell. She was a homemaker and also had owned and operated the first store in Helen called The Poor Petunia Antiques and Gifts.

Edmond F. Jared, Sr.

Edmond F. Jared, Sr., proudly served in the Army Air Force during World War II as a command pilot flying The Hump between India and China. He continued his military career, serving in the Air Force Reserve until his retirement in 1963. Edmond was very active in civic affairs and served as President of the Gainesville, Georgia, Chamber of Commerce. He culminated his career as a food broker for the military around the world.

The Jared Line

Nan's brothers:

Edmond Feris, Jr., Jerry Harrell, and David James

1920-2012 – Nan's Father: Edmond Feris Jared

1897-1947 - Grandfather: Marvin Wilcox Jared

1864-1946 - 1st Great Grandfather: James Allison Jared

1827-1903 - 2nd Great Grandfather: Moses Alexander Jared, Jr.

1790-1827 - 3rd Great Grandfather: Moses Alexander Jared

1791-1872 - 4th Great Grandfather: William Jared

1760-1835 - 5th Great Grandfather: Joseph Jackson Jared

1737-1804 - 6th Great Grandfather: John Kinchin Jared

1720-1753 - 7th Great Grandfather: Thomas J. Jarrell

1678-1741 - 8th Great Grandfather: Thomas Jarrett

1638-1686 - 9th Great Grandfather: Col. Thomas Gerard, Jr.

1608-1673 - 10th Great Grandfather: Sir, Dr. Thomas Gerard

Introduction

I joined a group of friends in Williamsburg, Virginia, to look into the history of our families. I told my friends the one question I wanted an answer to was why I had never known anyone outside of my direct family, who had my last name "Jared."

I've moved around quite a bit, but have not found any surname Jareds in Gainesville, Atlanta, Washington DC, or Maryland and Virginia. My grandfather Marvin Wilcox had two brothers in California, but that was it. Never did I know or meet anyone else with my same last name.

About 40 years ago, it became a popular boy's first name.

I set out to trace the Jared men all the way back to the first one to cross the Atlantic Ocean. I started with my grandfather, and using genealogy websites, worked backwards from son, to father, to father, and so on. Then, lo and behold, I found the first to cross over to this land in 1634.

His name was Sir Thomas Gerard, a surgeon from Lancastershire, England. He was sent by the House of Burgesses to help set up the first settlement in Maryland, St. Mary's. For me and my brothers, he would be our 10th great-Grandfather. The name was not spelled Jared then; that spelling was introduced in the early 1700's and has remained the same all the way down to Dylan and Faye. I have been told that in

England, "Gerard" is pronounced exactly the same way we pronounce "Jared."

I have gathered a wealth of information about the 11 men who brought the Jared name down to us...their wives, children, occupations, places they lived, and other fascinating details.

My father, Edmond Feris Jared, is not included because we all have the story of his life in his wonderful book, *One Hell of a Ride*.

This was a labor of love for all of you in the Jared family! I do hope that someone will pick up where this leaves off and trace the Gerard line in England back through the centuries.

Marvin Wilcox Jared

Grandfather

Date & Place of Birth: 1897—Pettis County, Missouri

Date & Place of Death: 1947—New Orleans, Louisiana

Parents: James Allison and Lillian Wilcox Jared

1st Wife: Minnie Lucille Feris (married 1917; divorced 1936)

    1 Child

2nd Wife: Dorothy

    1 Child

Marvin Wilcox Jared, later nicknamed "Jerry," was born in Sedalia, Pettis County, Missouri in 1897. He was the son of a Methodist Episcopal minister and was named after a famous Missouri Bishop, Enoch Mather Marvin. His middle name was the maiden name of his mother.

Marvin Wilcox, circa 1900

Marvin Wilcox

He became a camera fiend as a youngster and kept himself in pocket money photographing his friends. He went to Missouri State Teacher's College where he was a sprinter on the track team and sang in the college glee club. He also studied violin and voice for eight years. Photography was his chosen line of work.

Marvin Wilcox Jared

Minnie Lucille Feris Jared

In March 1917, he enlisted in the Missouri National Guard in Sedalia and helped to organize a machine gun company. A month later, his unit was ordered to Fort Sill, Oklahoma. On Christmas Eve of that year, he married Minnie Lucille Feris who had come to Fort Sill from Sedalia. They spent three weeks together and then did not see each other again for 22 months.

He left for overseas and was sent to a machine gun school in Chatillon-Sur-Seine where he served as an instructor for French soldiers.

Jerry with his mother Lillian Wilcox Jared

Jerry spent 13 months in France, came back to America in 1919, and moved to Monroe, Louisiana, where he started his own photography studio. His first son, Edmond Feris, was born there in 1920. He and his wife opened three more studios and then lost all their money during the Great Depression.

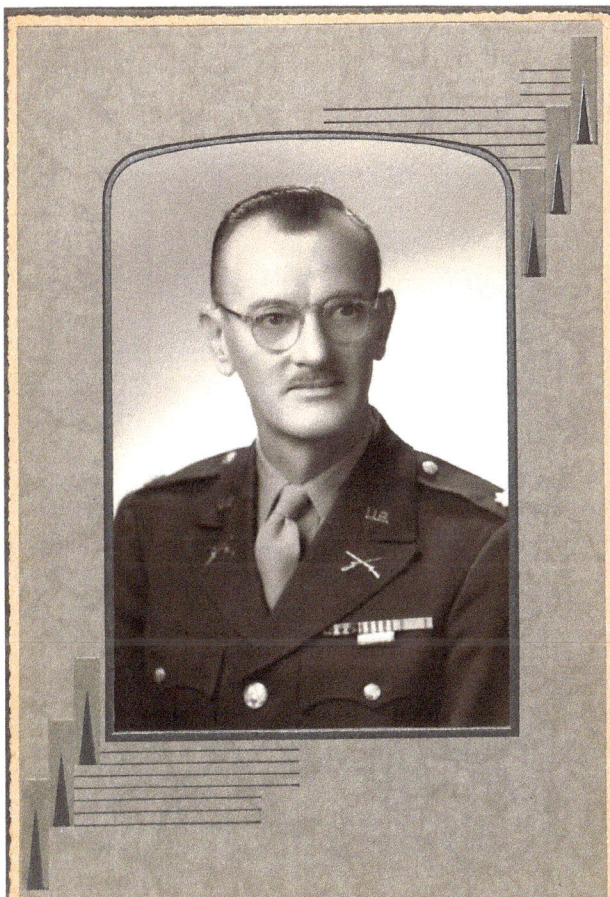

Lt Col Marvin Wilcox Jared

In 1929, he was commissioned in the Officers Reserve Corps and spent five 6-month tours as a Civilian Conservation Corps officer. In 1938 he resigned and became staff photographer for Louisiana State University. He was re-commissioned in the Army for World War II and became a Lieutenant Colonel.

Minnie and Jerry divorced. Minnie moved to Jacksonville, Florida and used her middle name "Lucille" from that time on.

Jerry then married Dorothy, and they had their son Frederick.

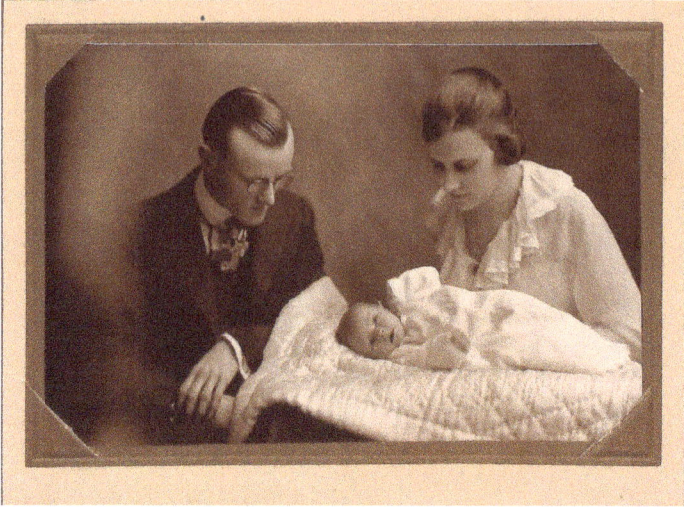

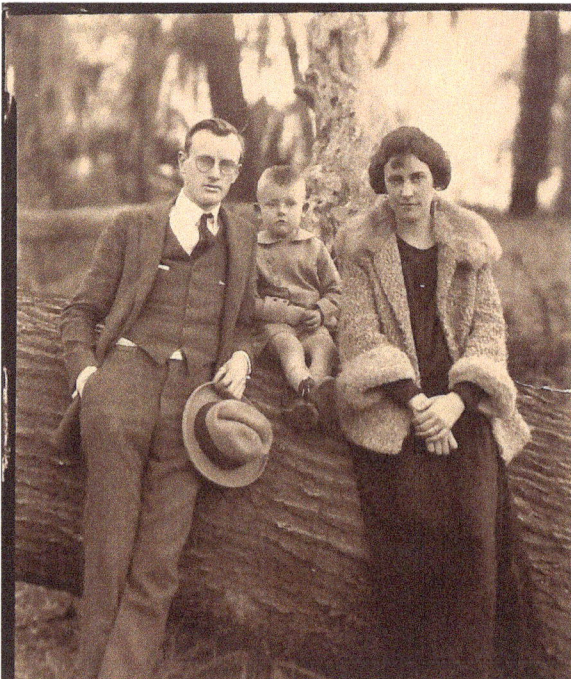

Jerry moved to New Orleans and died there in 1947 in a small pink house in The French Quarter.

Dumaine Street, New Orleans, Lousiana

He was buried in the Baton Rouge National Cemetery.

Baton Rouge National Cemetery,
East Baton Rouge, Louisiana

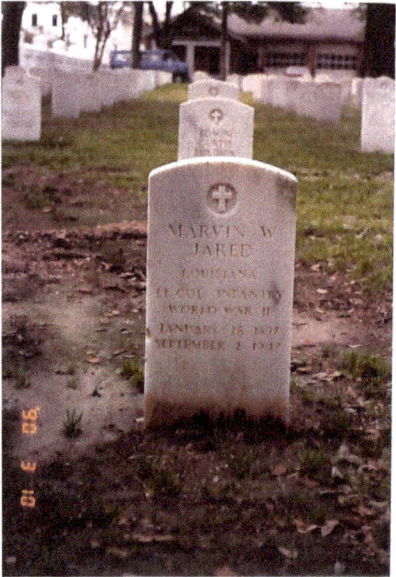

James Allison Jared

1ˢᵗ Great Grandfather

Date & Place of Birth: 1864—Pettis County, Missouri

Date & Place of Death: 1946—in Louisiana. Buried in Springfield, Missouri

Parents: Moses Alexander and Sarah Jared

Wife: Lillian Ethel Wilcox (divorced 1930)

  3 Children

James Allison was born in Missouri but grew up in Putnam County, Tennessee. At some point, he moved to Sedalia, Pettis County, Missouri where he met and married Lillian Ethel Wilcox.

James Allison

Lillian Wilcox

They had three sons: Marvin Wilcox, Porter Alexander, and Daniel Wade.

Lillian, James, Marvin and Porter

Lillian Wilcox Jared

James was a Methodist Episcopal minister who recorded and solemnized 119 marriages in Missouri. The book with the marriage certificates is with Todd Alexander, son of Porter Alexander, in Santa Barbara, California. Todd's grandfather was Marvin Wilcox's brother and represents another leg of the Jared line.

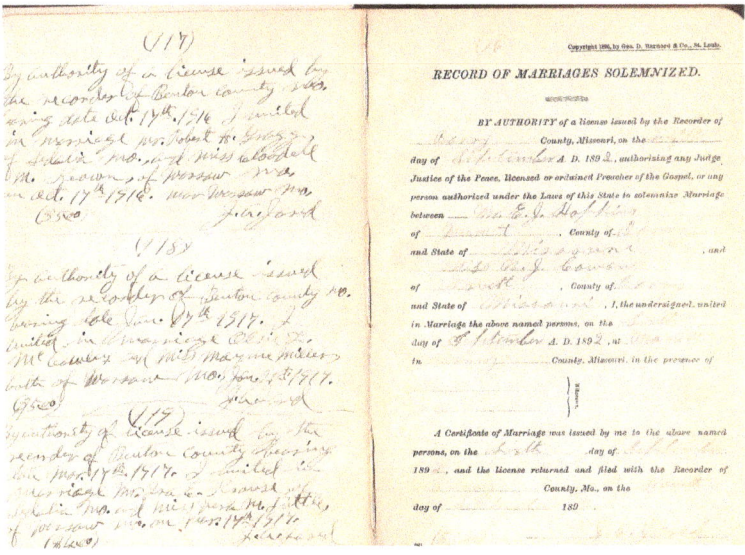

Methodist Episcopal Record Book

In 1930, James and Lillian divorced. She remained in Sedalia, and he moved to Springfield, Missouri. Before his death he moved to Louisiana to be with his son, Marvin (Jerry) Wilcox. He was taken back to Springfield to be buried in Maple Park Cemetery.

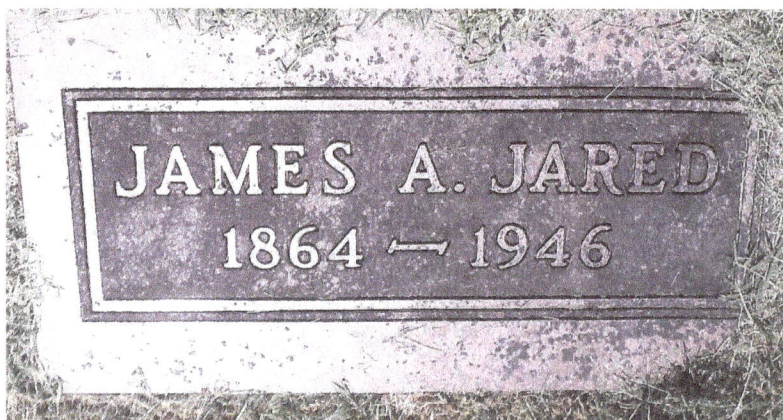

Moses Alexander Jared, Jr.

2nd Great Grandfather

Date & Place of Birth: 1827—Putnam County, Tennessee

Date & Place of Death: Died: 1903—Howell County, Missouri. Buried: Putnam County, Tennessee

Parents: Moses Alexander and Malinda Byrne

1st Wife: Maranda Jane Price

    13 Children

2nd Wife: Sarah Arena Thompson

    7 Children

Moses Alexander, Jr. was born four months after his father died. Superstition grew up around him. As a grown man, it was believed he had supernatural powers of healing. People would bring babies and ask him to blow in their mouths for sore throat or thrush.

He was the father of 13 children with his first wife, Maranda Jane Price. After her death, he married Sarah Arena Thompson, and they had seven children.

He and many in the family moved to Cureall, Missouri, a community east of Springfield. It was named Cureall after a mineral spring located there believed to have medicinal qualities.

Moses Alexander, Jr., and grandson LeRoy

He died in Missouri but was taken back to Tennessee to be buried.

Jesse Taylor, Moses Alexander, and Sarah Arena Thompson Jared tombstone in Tennessee.

Moses Alexander Jared, Sr.

3rd Great Grandfather

Date & Place of Birth: 1794—Bedford County, Virginia

Date & Place of Death: 1827—Putnam County, Tennessee

Parents: William and Polly Ralston

1st Wife: Malinda Byrne

      6 Children

2nd Wife: Margaret Turner

Except for the vital information above, almost nothing could be found about the first Moses Alexander. He was born in Virginia but moved to Tennessee with his parents and others in the Jared family. He married Malinda Byrne, and they had six children. After she died, he married Margaret Turner.

He was a very poor Presbyterian minister and lost four sons to winter fever.

William Jared

4ᵗʰ Great Grandfather

Date & Place of Birth: 1791—Bedford County, Virginia

Date & Place of Death: 1872—Putnam County, Tennessee

Parents: Joseph Jackson and Martha Agnes (Aggie) Beard

Wife: Martha (Polly) Ralston

    5 Children

William was born in Bedford Country, Virginia (where Roanoke is now).

He married Polly Ralston in 1808, and they moved to Putnam County, Tennessee to join other family Jareds. Joseph and Polly had five children.

William was a farmer and bought land worth $2,000 in Jacksonville, Morgan County, Illinois, just west of Springfield. He was elected coroner at age 37 and served in the Illinois militia.

He moved back to Tennessee later in life and died there.

Joseph Jackson Jared

5th Great Grandfather

Date & Place of Birth: 1760—Kingswood, New Jersey

Date & Place of Death: 1835—Putnam County, Tennessee: Quaker Colony

Parents: John Kinchin and Hannah Whitacre

1st wife: Martha Agnes Beard

    7 Children

2nd wife: Elizabeth Baker

    9 Children

Joseph Jackson was born in a Quaker community in New Jersey but moved to Loudoun County, Virginia (where Leesburg is now) as a very young child. His first wife was Martha Agnes "Aggie" Beard. She died young after bearing seven children. He then married Elizabeth "Bessie" Baker, and together they had nine more children.

He and his brother William enlisted in the Revolutionary Army (Russell's Virginia regiment) in 1779 at Lucy's Tavern on Bulskin Creek in Loudoun County. He marched to Richmond and other places in Virginia but was discharged after three months. He reenlisted in the summer of 1781 and fought in the Battle of Little York (Yorktown) under George Washington.

Joseph Jackson was due a pension for his service in the war. He had trouble getting it because he had no papers. When he finally received it, the sum was $20 per annum.

Joseph Jackson moved his family to Bedford Country, Virginia (where Roanoke is now) in the 1780s.

He and his brother William were given land bounty grants. From 1795 to 1810, most of the Jared family moved to the wilderness of Tennessee. Each was given 50 acres, and they settled on a farm on a ridge known as Low Gap, Tennessee. This land is now a part of Putnam County.

John Kinchin Jared

6th Great Grandfather

Date & Place of Birth: 1737—Isle of Wight, Virginia

Date & Place of Death: 1804—Falls Township, Wyoming County, Pennsylvania

Parents: Thomas and Martha Kinchin

1st Wife: Hannah Whitacre

> 3 Children

2nd Wife: Rachel Palmer

> 10 Children

John was born in Isle of Wight, Virginia, the only child of Thomas and Martha Kinchin. There he met his first wife Hannah Whitacre who was a Quaker. They moved to Pennsylvania, then settled in New Jersey to be part of Quaker Communities. They moved back to John's birth state and settled in Loudoun County, Virginia.

John was a wagon maker and storekeeper. He lived in the period and area that developed the Conestoga wagon. Scores of pioneers in these wagons passed John's store as they travelled hundreds of miles through the wilderness.

John and Hannah had two boys and one girl. In 1765, she passed away, leaving him to manage the three children alone.

He married Rachel Palmer two years later, and together, they had ten children.

When the War for Independence came, John was torn between the Quaker learnings and his duty to home and country. When the Jared home was threatened, John and his two oldest boys, Joseph and William, marched away to defend it.

Thomas J. Jarrell, Thomas IV

7ʰ Great Grandfather

Date & Place of Birth: 1720—Dinwiddy County, Virginia

Date & Place of Death: 1753—Isle of Wight, Virginia

Parents: Thomas Jared III and Sarah Hardy

Wife: Martha Kinchin

   1 Child: John

Thomas IV was born in Dinwiddie, County, Virginia. His family moved to Isle of Wight, Virginia in Southampton County.

He married his wife Martha Kinchin in 1734, and they had only one son, John, when Thomas was 17 years old.

Thomas was a member of the House of Burgesses in Southampton County, which at the time included the Isle of Wight settlement. The House of Burgesses continued the Parliament system in what was then English America. Documents show that he examined estates, appraised estates, and was the executor of his wife's father's estate.

At some point, the spelling of his name found in the legal documents was changed to Jarrell.

He died in Isle of Wight, Virginia at the early age of 33. His wife, Martha Kinchin, died even younger at only 31.

Thomas Jared III (Jarrett)

8ᵗʰ Great Grandfather

Date & Place of Birth: 1668—St. Mary's, Maryland

Date & Place of Death: 1741—Isle of Wight, Virginia

Parents: Thomas Gerard, Jr. and Ann Smallwood Hawkins

Wife: Sarah Hardy

    2 Children

Thomas Jarrett III was born in St. Mary's County, Maryland in 1668. He married Sarah Hardy in 1697.

At some point, they moved to the settlement of Isle of Wight, Virginia, located across the James River from Jamestown. There is no information to explain why they moved, but it could be due to the differences with his family over the inheritance from his grandfather to his father that never took place.

Thomas III and Sarah moved to Dinwiddie County, Virginia where their son Thomas IV was born in 1720. The family moved back to Isle of Wight where Thomas III died in 1741.

There are documents that show he was an appraiser, and in these documents, his name is spelled "Jarrett."

Colonel Thomas Gerard, Jr.

9ᵗʰ Great Grandfather

Date & Place of Birth: 1638—St. Mary's County, Virginia

Date & Place of Death: 1686—St. Mary's County, Virginia

Wife: Ann Smallwood Hawkins

    2 Children

Thomas Gerard II was born in England and moved with his family to join his father in St. Mary's County, Maryland in 1650. He married Elizabeth Ann Smallwood Hawkins, and they had two children. Thomas spent most of his life in Maryland, but after this mother died, probably spent time across the Potomac in Virginia.

He was a merchant and an attorney. He also served as a factor, or an agent acting on behalf of others. He held the offices of Justice, Coroner, and Appraiser.

Following his father's death, the younger Thomas Gerard was forced to sue his stepmother Rose and her son John Gerard for failing to settle the elder Gerard's estate and ignoring an earlier agreement between father and son. In 1677, the Provincial Court found in favor of Rose's son John.

In 1672, his father sold him two tracts of land in Clement's Manor totaling 2,000 acres. The remaining land was split between his eldest brother Justinian and Rose's son John. Nothing more was left to him in his father's will.

Sir Thomas Gerard

10th Great Grandfather

Date & Place of Birth: 1608—Newell, Lancastershire, England

Date & Place of Death: 1673—Westmoreland County, Virginia

Parents: John and Frances Molyneux

1st Wife: Lady Susannah Snow

   8 Children

2nd Wife: Rose Tucker

   1 Child

Thomas Gerard was born in 1608 in Lancastershire, England. His father was part of a prominent Roman Catholic family that has been traced back to the time of the General Survey of the Kingdom in 1078. He became a surgeon and married Susannah Snowe in 1634.

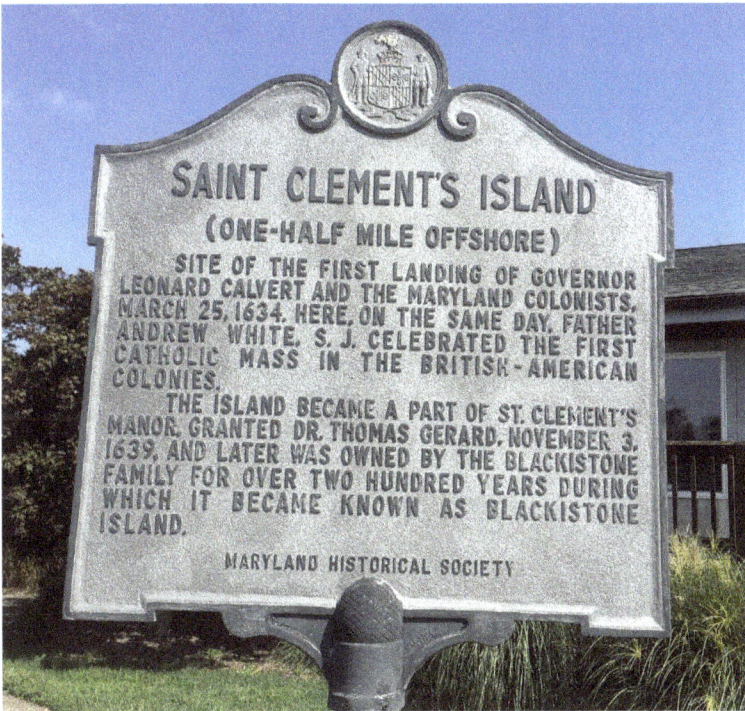

SAINT CLEMENT'S ISLAND
(ONE-HALF MILE OFFSHORE)

SITE OF THE FIRST LANDING OF GOVERNOR LEONARD CALVERT AND THE MARYLAND COLONISTS, MARCH 25, 1634. HERE, ON THE SAME DAY, FATHER ANDREW WHITE, S. J. CELEBRATED THE FIRST CATHOLIC MASS IN THE BRITISH-AMERICAN COLONIES.

THE ISLAND BECAME A PART OF ST. CLEMENT'S MANOR, GRANTED DR. THOMAS GERARD, NOVEMBER 3, 1639, AND LATER WAS OWNED BY THE BLACKISTONE FAMILY FOR OVER TWO HUNDRED YEARS DURING WHICH IT BECAME KNOWN AS BLACKISTONE ISLAND.

MARYLAND HISTORICAL SOCIETY

Thomas's first visit to Maryland was in 1638 when he arrived on one of two ships, the Ark or the Dove. Others had arrived four years earlier and established the colony of Maryland. Their first landing was on St. Clement's Island, and the St. Mary's settlement on the mainland became Maryland's first capital.

Thomas had been selected by the Lord Baltimore of England to begin the "Manor System" in Maryland and was issued one of the first manorial grants. This was a patent for 1,030 acres, which he called St. Clement's Manor. It included the island where the first colonists landed.

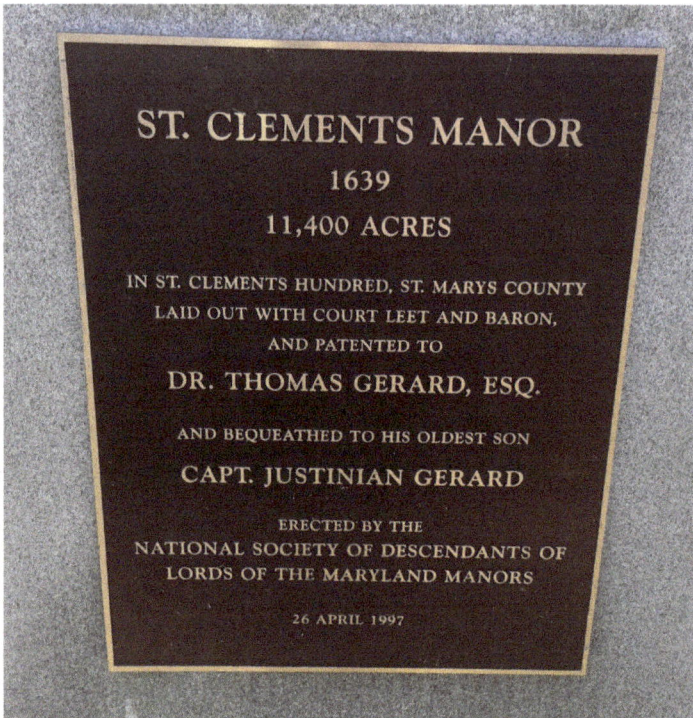

He sold his property in England and brought over his family and 40 servants. He continued to acquire property, and at the time of his death, he owned 16,000 acres in Maryland and Virginia, across the Potomac River.

Because Thomas's wife Susannah and the children were Protestant, he erected an Anglican chapel on St. Clement's Manor in 1642. This later became the All Saint's Episcopal Church. While it is no longer functioning, the present church dates to 1846.

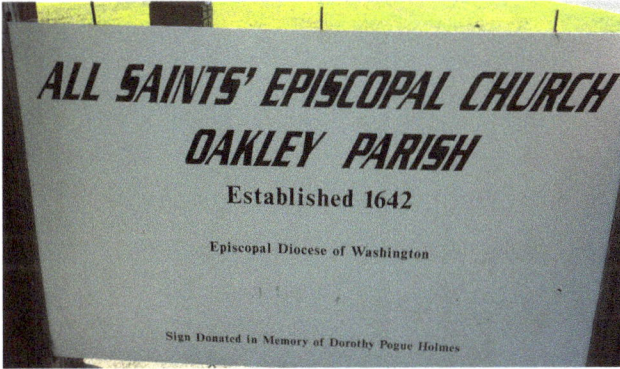

ALL SAINTS' EPISCOPAL CHURCH
OAKLEY PARISH

Established 1642

Episcopal Diocese of Washington

Sign Donated in Memory of Dorothy Pogue Holmes

He and Susannah had six daughters and three sons. Susannah died in 1666 and was buried at St. Clement's Manor. After her death, he spent most of the rest of his life at his place in Virginia called "Gerard's Reserve."

He married a widow, Rose Tucker Thomas, but when near death, requested to be returned to Maryland and be buried next to his first wife Susannah. The Gerard family cemetery in St. Mary's County was on land overlooking the Potomac. However, due to a terrible storm, the land gave way and washed away into the river.

Your AncestryDNA Results reveal your unique story —
who your ancestors were and where they came from.

Results as of:
12 Dec 2018

DNA Results Summary for Nan Jared Powell

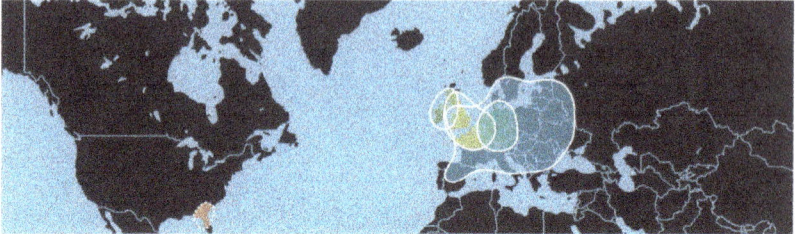

© Mapbox, © OpenStreetMap

Ethnicity Estimate

England, Wales & Northwestern Europe	69%
Ireland & Scotland	25%
Germanic Europe	3%
Sweden	2%
European Jewish	1%
Finland	<1%

Migrations

Georgia & Florida Settlers
- North & Central Florida Settlers
- Southeast Georgia Settlers
- South Carolina, Georgia & Northeast Florida Coast Settlers

About the Author

Nan Jared Powell was raised in Gainesville, Georgia. She attended Brenau College to get her teaching degree. After graduation, she moved to Atlanta to teach elementary school. Her passion for teaching kept her in the classroom for 22 years.

She spent over 30 years in Washington DC with her husband, Jody Powell. After his death in 2009, she settled in Williamsburg, Virginia to be close to family.

She is continuing her enthusiasm for teaching by sharing her genealogy with her family in *The Jared Line*.

To learn more about Nan's father, Edmond F. Jared, check out his memoir, *One Hell of a Ride*.

Ranging from above the Himalayan Mountains to the beginnings of Lake Lanier in Georgia, from solitude of solo flight to the fellowship of family life and civic organizations, and from the discipline of the military to the ever-changing world of business, Ed Jared gives us one "Greatest Generation" perspective on his experience of the twentieth century as he tells us the story of his rich and fascinating life. His life was *One Hell of a Ride.*

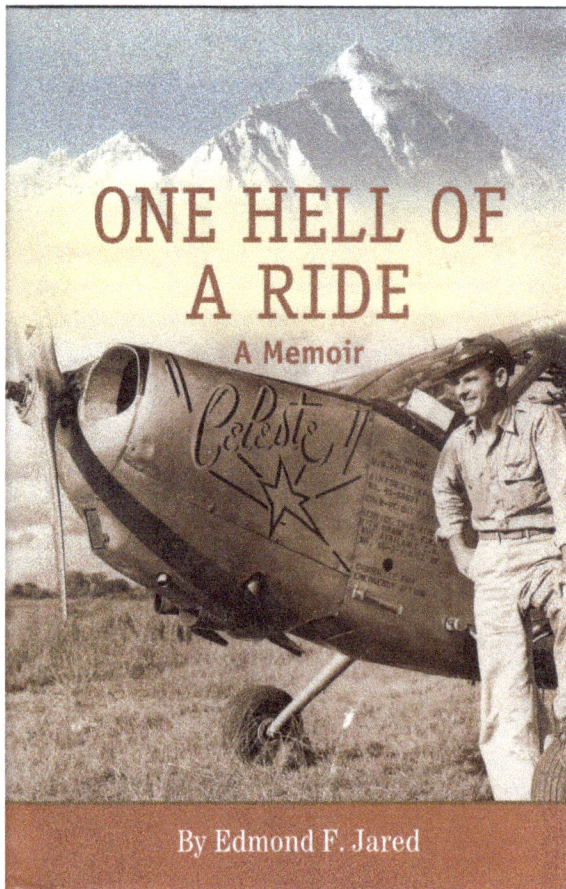

www.ingramcontent.com/pod-product-compliance
Lightning Source LLC
Chambersburg PA
CBHW041929260326
41914CB00009B/1235